1 MONTH OF
FREE
READING

at

www.ForgottenBooks.com

By purchasing this book you are eligible for one month membership to ForgottenBooks.com, giving you unlimited access to our entire collection of over 1,000,000 titles via our web site and mobile apps.

To claim your free month visit:

www.forgottenbooks.com/free903022

ISBN 978-0-266-87605-2
PIBN 10903022

istoric, archived docume

t assume content reflects c
c knowledge, policies, or pr

62183

STOCK IN CANS · LINERS · VINES · SHRUBS · TREES

JUNIPERS ARBORVITAES · BROADLEAFS

VERHALEN

WHOLESALE PRICE LIST

Fall 1950 - Spring 1951

VERHALEN NURSERY CO.

SCOTTSVILLE, TEXAS

and

1114 South Beckley
DALLAS 8, TEXAS

Your Profits Grow in Verhalen Plants

POLICY—

Our policy is to furnish stock fully graded and properly named. Any deviation from this plan will be accidental and we assume no responsibility greater than the invoice amount of the stock involved.

TERMS—

ALL SALES ARE STRICTLY CASH with the one exception of those whose credit has been established in past years. NO DISCOUNTS. Nursery supplies are cash to every one alike.

CLAIMS—

Our responsibility for condition of plants being shipped ends when we make delivery in good order to the transporting companies. Damages inflicted thereafter are to be taken up with the carrier. We will assist when we can help in settling such problems.

Claims for quality of stock must be made within 10 days after date of invoice. LATE CLAIMS WILL NOT BE CONSIDERED.

PACKING CHARGES AND TRUCK DELIVERIES—

Baling, boxing or crating for local freight or express shipments will be charged at cost. No charges are made for bulk truck or car loading.

Deliveries to customers in Dallas on invoices of $50 or over will be made on our truck at F.O.B. Dallas Warehouse prices.

To other destinations where two or more orders are delivered in the same load each customer will be charged proportionately as to mileage and size of his order.

DELIVERY CHARGES PAYABLE AT TIME OF DELIVERY.

ORDERS—

All orders are accepted with the understanding that we are not to be held liable in event of accidents, extremities of weather or other causes beyond our control.

Prices herein cancel all previous listings. We reserve the right to alter prices at any time.

Season of 1950 - 1951

⌒

VERHALEN NURSERY COMPANY
SCOTTSVILLE, TEXAS

TELEPHONE   TELEGRAMS
Marshall, Texas, 4876   Western Union, Scottsville, Texas

Geo. F. Verhalen, Pres.   R. P. Verhalen, Vice-Pres.
Tel. Marshall 4866   Tel. Marshall 4831

Steve G. Verhalen, Sec'y and Sales
Tel. Marshall 5898

ADDRESS ALL CORRESPONDENCE
TO SCOTTSVILLE, TEXAS

⌒

Dallas Warehouse

Verhalen Nursery Company

C. P. HARRIS, Mgr.

Phone Y8-9876

1114 S. Beckley — Dallas 8, Texas

⌒

Prices are for bulk truck and carloading. Packaging of freight and express shipments at cost. Truckloads will be delivered up to approximately 400 miles from nursery at a low mileage charge. Not responsible for unfilled orders by causes beyond our control.

AUTO ROUTE

Wholesale Only—No Retail Sales

⌒

Members of Leading National and State
Nursery Associations

QUALITY LINERS

Only the best of parent stock, is used in our propagation of liners. Constant care is exercised throughout the production period and in packing for shipment. This guarantees that our customers receive only the best of plants and that they arrive in first class condition.

No additional charges will be made for packing of liners, when 50 or more of a variety are ordered. For less than 50 of a size, add 10% to amount of purchase.

Bareroot liners are packed in sphagnum moss. Potted liners are removed from clay into paper pots and also wrapped in paper before being crated.

Verhalen liners are grown in deep 2½ in. pots in outdoor beds. Our potted liners do not have to wait for favorable weather to be moved. They are always ready to go. The larger pot means a bigger plant. The outdoor treatment avoids any possibility of shock in transplanting.

BLUESPIRE ARBORVITAE - SPINY GREEK
EXCELSA ARBORVITAE - IRISH JUNIPER

LINING OUT LIST

C denotes cutting grown and S denotes seedling grown.

VARIETY		Bareroot	Pots
Biota Baker	C	.10	.15
Biota Berckmanns	C	.13	.18
Biota Bluespire	C	.12	.17
Biota Bonita	C	.12	—
Biota Bonita Golden	C	.12	—
Biota Excelsa	C	.10	—
Biota Goldcone	C	—	.17
Boxwood, Harland	C	.10	—
Cherry Laurel	S	.06	.15
Eleagnus Macrophylla	C	—	.18
Eleagnus Simoni	C	.13	.18
Euonymus Japonica	C	—	.13
Euonymus Patens	C	—	.10
Gardenia Fortunei	C	—	.10
Gelsemium Sempervirens	C	.10	.15
Holly, Burfordi	C	.13	.18

MAGNOLIA GRANDIFLORA - EUONYMUS PATENS
ILEX CORNUTA - PFITZER JUNIPER

VARIETY		Bareroot	Pots
Holly, Cornuta	C	—	.20
Holly, Crenata Rotundifolia	C	—	.16
Honeysuckle Magnifica	C	.10	—
Juniper, Ashford	C	.10	.15
Juniper, Irish	C	.08	.13
Juniper Irish extra heavy	C	—	.15
Juniper, Kiyono	C	.10	.15
Juniper, Pfitzer	C	.13	.18
Juniper, Procumbens	C	.12	.17
Juniper, Spiny Greek	C	.13	.18
Juniper, Sylvestris	C	.13	.18
Juniper, Vaseshape	C	.08	.13
Juniper, Vonehron	C	—	.15
Loropetalum Chinensis	C	—	.15
Magnolia grandiflora	S	—	.15
Mahonia bealei	S	—	.15
Mimosa, Pink	S	.05	—
Mimosa, White	S	.06	—

PROPAGATING HOUSE—POT PLANT SECTION

VARIETY		Bareroot	Pots
Photenia ....S		—	.15
Pyracantha-Barlow-Red C		—	.17
Pyracantha-Graber-Red C		—	.17
Pyracantha-Henderson-Red C		—	.17
Pyracantha Miller-Red C		—	.17
Pyracantha Laland-Orange C		—	.14
Red Bud, American ....S		.06	—
Red Bud, Chinese ....S		.08	—
Spirea Reevesi ....S		.08	—

Please remember Verhalen Liners are larger because they are grown in larger pots.

CONIFERS

ALL PLANTS ARE BALLED & BURLAPPED WHERE WEIGHT IS SHOWN. WITHOUT WEIGHT THEY ARE BAREROOT.

Biota orientalis............DWARF GOLDEN ARBORVITAE

A compact grower; is smaller, more brilliant and more uniformly golden than Berckmanns. Hardy. 4 feet.

	Weight	10 or More F.O.B. Nursery	F.O.B. Dallas Less than 10 at Nursery
15-18 in. 22		$1.00	$1.10
18-24 in. 30		1.50	1.65
24-30 in. 40		2.00	2.20

Biota orientalis aurea nana............................BERCKMANNS GOLDEN ARBORVITAE

Very compact and moderately slow in growth. New foliage is golden. 15 feet.

15-18 in. 22	1.00	1.10
18-24 in. 30	1.50	1.65
24-30 in. 40	2.00	2.20

Biota orientalis bonita....................BONITA ARBORVITAE

Dwarf size, rich dark green color, compact and round character. 4 feet.

15-18 in. 22	1.00	1.10
18-24 in. 30	1.50	1.65

Biota orientalis............GOLDEN BONITA ARBORVITAE

Golden form of Bonita Arborvitae. Color is just as good as Dwarf Golden Arborvitae. 4 feet.

15-18 in. 22	1.10	1.20
18-24 in. 40	1.60	1.75

Biota orientalis excelsa................EXCELSA ARBORVITAE

A very hardy and cold resistant type having broader base and darker color than Baker Arborvitae and equally at home in either the north or south. Particularly well suited for Oklahoma, Kansas and Missouri. 8 feet.

1 gallon 8	.45	.50
18-24 in. 30	1.00	1.10
24-30 in. 40	1.40	1.55
30-36 in. 40	1.75	1.90
3-4 ft. 70	2.25	2.45

Biota orientalis howardi........BLUESPIRE ARBORVITAE
More columnar and darker than Baker Arborvitae. Bluish foliage
prompts its name. Keeps its good color during dry or cold
weather. 10 feet.

	Weight	10 or More F.O.B. Nursery	F.O.B. Dallas Less than 10 at Nursery
18-24 in.	.30	1.00	1.10
24-30 in.	.40	1.40	1.55
30-36 in.	.40	1.75	1.90
3 - 4 ft.	.70	2.25	2.45
4 - 5 ft.	.110	2.75	3.00

BAKER ARBORVITAE - I gallon

Biota orientalis pyramidalis................BAKER'S HYBRID
ARBORVITAE
Pyramidal, compact and fast grower. Light green color. 15 feet.

1 gallon	8	.50	.55
18-24 in.	.30	1.00	1.10
24-30 in.	.40	1.40	1.55
30-36 in.	.40	1.75	1.90
3 - 4 ft.	.70	2.25	2.45

Biota orientalis.........................ROSEDALE ARBORVITAE
Steel blue color foliage. Plant grows very compact and shapely
without shearing. Texture of foliage is fine and feathery.
Grading this year will be generous due to good growing
conditions. 8 feet.

1 gallon	8	.45	.50

Biota orientalis aurea conspicua.......................GOLDSPIRE
ARBORVITAE
Conspicuously golden color on very flat panels. Growth is
pyramidal and open. 20 feet.

18-24 in.	.30	1.10	1.20
24-30 in.	.40	1.50	1.65

Cedrus deodara.........................DEODAR OR HIMALAYAN
CEDAR
Most graceful evergreen tree for the south. 30 feet.

1 gallon	8	.60	.65
5 gallon	35	1.60	1.75

Cupressus arizonica.............................ARIZONA CYPRESS
Pyramidal growing conifer. Rather slender in shape and has
silvery light blue foliage. A fast grower, a good seller on the
sales yard. 25 feet.

1 gallon	8	.50	.55

Cupressus sempervirens........................ITALIAN CYPRESS

Narrow, with branches tight against main stem; dark green foliage. B&B plants are cutting grown, assuring uniformity. 35 feet.

	Weight	10 or More F.O.B. Nursery	F.O.B. Dallas Less than 10 at Nursery
1 gallon	8	.45	.50
30-36 in.	30	1.20	1.30
3 - 4 ft.	40	1.60	1.75

Libocedrus decurrens compacta............DWARF INCENSE CEDAR

Broad, flat, fan shaped Arborvitae-like foliage. Dark green, having strong cedar fragrance.

5 gallon	35	1.50	1.65

—

JUNIPERS

Juniperus chinensis pfitzeriana............PFITZER JUNIPER

These are not two or three branched plants. They are well developed, full bodied, high crowned stock due to heavy shearing.

15-18 in.	22	1.50	1.65
18-24 in.	30	2.00	2.20

Juniperus chinensis densa glauca............DWARF GREEK JUNIPER

Heavy blue-green foliage on pyramidal shape; varying length stems giving an overall irregular but well balanced form. A valuable and dependable plant. Very adaptable to Gulf Coast Area. 10 feet.

15-18 in.	22	1.25	1.35
18-24 in.	30	1.50	1.65

Juniperus chinensis sylvestris........SYLVESTER JUNIPER

Its special attraction is its soft green two types of foliage and thickly covered irregular side branches. 25 feet.

1 gallon	8	.50	.55
24-30 in.	30	1.50	1.65
30-36 in.	40	1.85	2.00
3 - 4 ft.	70	2.50	2.75

Juniperus communis ashfordi............ASHFORD JUNIPER

A fast growing plant most useful in hedging because of its compactness, broadness, and straight sides. Also its inexpensiveness makes it very convenient for competitive real estate plantings. 10 feet.

1 gallon	8	.40	.45
18-24 in.	30	1.00	1.10
24-30 in.	30	1.35	1.50
30-36 in.	40	1.60	1.75
15-18 in. sheared globes	30	1.10	1.20
18-24 in. sheared globes	40	1.45	1.60

Juniperus communis depressa vase shape....VASE SHAPE JUNIPER

New, symmetrically bowl-shaped. Does not sunburn. 4 feet.

15-18 in.	22	.80	.90
18-24 in.	30	1.20	1.30

Juniperus communis hibernica fastigiata..................IRISH JUNIPER

An exceedingly narrow form of upright pillar-like juniper which is weather and sun-resistant and does well in our southwest. 8 feet.

1 gallon	8	.45	.50
5 gallon	35	1.20	1.30
18-24 in.	30	1.20	1.30
24-30 in.	30	1.50	1.65
30-36 in.	40	1.85	2.00

Juniperus communis columnaris kiyonoi.................**KIYONO JUNIPER**

Upright growing. Should be used for medium height columnar effects. Does not sunburn. 12 feet.

	Weight	10 or More F.O.B. Nursery	F.O.B. Dallas Less than 10 at Nursery
1 gallon	8	.60	.65
18-24 in.	30	1.00	1.10
24-30 in.	30	1.35	1.50
30-36 in.	40	1.60	1.75
24-30 in.	40	2.00	2.20

Juniper conferta..**SHORE JUNIPER**

Pleasing light green, soft foliage, not spiny; prostrate on ground; branchlets growing upright to 12 inches. Excellent for driveway entrance, hanging over walls, etc. 8 foot spread.

1 gallon	8	.50	.55

Juniperus excelsa stricta............**SPINY GREEK JUNIPER**

Small, conical glaucous tree. 6 feet.

1 gallon	8	.60	.65
15-18 in.	22	1.25	1.35
18-24 in.	30	1.50	1.60
24-30 in.	40	2.00	2.20

Juniperus procumbens.......................**JAPANESE JUNIPER**

Low, creeping plant with thick blue-green foliage. Upright trained specimens are grown on a single straight stem with all the spread above the ground. They stand without support when ready to sell. A most novel plant. 10 foot spread.

15-18 in. spreading	30	1.25	1.35
2-3 ft. Upright trained	70	4.00	4.50
3-4 ft. Upright trained	110	5.00	5.50

Juniperus sabina...**SAVIN JUNIPER**

Light green foliage growing upright into low vase shape with tips inclined to curve downward. Very graceful and effective for low plantings. 4 foot spread.

18-24 in.	40	2.00	2.20
24-30 in.	40	2.50	2.75
30-36 in.	70	3.00	3.30

Juniperus sabina tamariscifolia..........**TAMARIX LEAVED SAVIN JUNIPER**

Dark green foliage. Grows in flat panels horizontally and close to the ground. It is the preferred flat juniper in some localities. 6 foot spread.

12-15 in.	22	1.10	1.20
15-18 in.	22	1.35	1.50

Juniperus sabina vonehron.............**VONEHRON JUNIPER**

A broad fast-growing form of Savin Juniper, having rich green foliage. 10 foot spread.

15-18 in.	22	1.50	1.65
18-24 in.	30	2.00	2.20
24-30 in.	40	2.50	2.75

Juniperus sabina vonhron....................**UPRIGHT TRAINED VONEHRON JUNIPER**

Uprightly trained Vonehron Juniper. An unusual new landscape form. Trained from 2 to 6 feet tall. Looks like and used as a dwarfed Canaert Juniper.

2-3 ft.	70	3.00	3.30
3-4 ft.	70	3.75	4.10
4-5 ft.	110	4.50	4.95
5-6 ft.	160	5.50	6.00

Juniperus squamata meyeri............**MEYER OR FISHTAIL JUNIPER**

A silvery-blue thick, heavily foliaged, odd, unevenly growing juniper; especially good for rock gardens or other important positions. Partial shade. Dwarf. 4 feet.

12-15 in.	22	1.25	1.35

Juniperus virginiana...RED CEDAR

An exceedingly comely form admired by all for its close, finely cut, smooth bright green foliage which also lends itself admirably to shearing. The pungent aroma of native cedar is very evident in this tree. 40 feet.

	Weight	10 or More F.O.B. Nursery	F.O.B. Dallas Less than 10 at Nursery
24-30 in. 40		1.50	1.65
30-36 in. 40		1.75	1.95
3-4 ft. 70		2.00	2.20
6-7 ft. 160		5.00	5.50
7-8 ft. 200		7.00	8.00
2-3 ft. Sheared standards 40		2.00	2.20
3-4 ft. Sheared standards 40		2.50	2.75
4-5 ft. Sheared standards 70		3.00	3.30
5-6 ft. Sheared standards 70		4.00	4.40

Pinus taeda...LOBLOLLY PINE

Native East Texas. Medium leaf yellow pine; stocky full young trees.

1 gallon 8		.40	.45
2-3 ft.—B&B 40		1.00	1.10
3-4 ft—B&B 70		1.50	1.65

ABELIA GRANDIFLORA - 5 gallon

BROADLEAVED EVERGREENS

ALL PLANTS ARE BALLED & BURLAPPED WHERE
WEIGHT IS SHOWN. WITHOUT WEIGHT THEY ARE
BAREROOT.

Abelia grandiflora..GLOSSY ABELIA

Shrub with dark green and coppery very glossy leaves and covered all summer with a myriad of fragrant dainty, light pinkish-white bell shaped flowers. 7 feet.

	Weight	10 or More F.O.B. Nursery	F.O.B. Dallas Less than 10 at Nursery
1 gallon	8	.50	.55
5 gallon	35	1.25	1.35
15-18 in.—1 yr.	22	.50	.55
18-24 in.—2 yr.	30	1.00	1.10
2-3 ft.—3 yr.	40	1.50	1.65
3-4 ft.— 3 yr.	70	2.00	2.20
4-5 ft.	110	3.00	3.30
5-6 ft.	110	4.00	4.40

Azalea indica..FORMOSA AZALEA

Larger and faster growing plant, larger leaves and flowers than the Kurume varieties and not so hardy. Its beauty is just as great however. For attracting customers, it is unexcelled. Purplish pink flowers.

9 -12 in.	8	.60	.65
12-15 in.	12	.80	.90
15-18 in.	18	1.00	1.10

Azalea indica..PRIDE OF MOBILE

Similar to Formosa in appearance and growth, however, flowers are lighter in color, being almost pure pink. Most popular of the Indica varieties.

9 -12 in.	8	.60	.65
12-15 in.	12	.80	.90
15-18 in.	18	1.00	1.10

Azalea kurume................................CORAL BELL AZALEA

Compact growing shrub; glossy leaves and dainty bell shaped, shell pink flowers, shading deeper at center; cover entire plant during flowering season.

6- 9 in.	8	.75	.80
9-12 in.	8	1.10	1.20
12-15 in.	12	1.35	1.50

Azalea kurume....................HINODEGIRI AZALEA

Slow grower but at blooming time solidly covered with brilliant scarlet flowers. The most popular red.

6 - 9 in.	8	.75	.80
9 -12 in.	8	1.10	1.20
12-15 in.	12	1.35	1.50

Berberis julianae................WINTERGREEN BARBERRY

Irregular shape bush with serrate edged medium green leaves and few spines; an unusual and useful broadleaf shrub. Formerly sold as Sargent Barberry. 6 feet.

1 gallon	8	.35	.40
12-15 in.	22	.60	.65
15-18 in.	22	.90	1.00

Berberis mentorensis........................MENTOR BARBERRY

A good evergreen shrub. Uniform dark green color. Branches are numerous and grow upright. Extremely suitable for hedge plantings. Grows in most any type soil.

1 gallon	8	.60	.65

Buxus harlandi..HARLAND BOXWOOD

Lighter color than regular boxwood, leaf is long and narrow and shrub is of dwarf habit. Suitable for edging and low borders. 3 feet.

1 gallon	8	.50	.55

Buxus sempervirens............................COMMON BOXWOOD

Small, smooth and slightly curved dark glossy green leaves growing as close to one another as it is possible for them to grow which
makes each plant a solid mass ideally suited to either specimen or
hedge use. True dwarf. The most popular variety. 6 feet.

	Weight	10 or More F.O.B. Nursery	F.O.B. Dallas Less than 10 at Nursery
1 gallon	8	.50	.55
10-12 in.	14	1.35	1.45
12-15 in.	22	1.60	1.75
15-18 in.	22	1.90	2.10

Camellia sasanqua..........................SASANQUA CAMELLIA

This is rapidly becoming an important plant in landscape design.
The leaves of the plant are dark and glossy. Cold Resistant. Shade
or sun is equally good for this hardy plant. A good flowering evergreen. 6 feet.

VARIETIES: CLEOPATRA: A more compact growing sasanqua than
most. Flowers are large, brilliant red and double.
MINE-NO-YUKI: A fast and open growth is nature of this plant.
Flowers are double pure white.
ROSEA: Upright graceful growth is character of this variety. Single
bright pink flowers cover it.

1 gallon	8	.70	.75
5 gallon	35	1.60	1.75
15-18 in.	22	1.50	1.65
18-24 in.	30	1.75	1.90

Elaeagnus macrophylla.............LONGLEAF ELAEAGNUS

Noble looking shrubs with varying degrees of color and character
of growth and foliage that adapts them to a broad field of usage.
12 feet.

18-24 in.	30	1.25	1.35
2 - 3 ft.	40	1.50	1.65
3 - 4 ft.	70	1.75	1.90

Elaeagnus pungens simoni...............SIMON ELAEAGNUS

Long and narrow leaves, grayish green over a silvery back. Medium
grower. 8 feet.

5 gallon	35	1.25	1.35
2 - 3 ft.	40	1.50	1.65

Euonymus japonica.....................EVERGREEN EUONYMUS

Bushy form with dark green oblong evenly notched leaves. Excellent for hedges. Most suitable in West Texas. 20 feet.

1 gallon	8	.40	.45
15-18 in.	22	.65	.70
18-24 in.	30	1.00	1.10

Feijoa sellowiana................................PINEAPPLE GUAVA

Grayish green shrub with blood red flowers and edible fruits.
Leaves are green above and gray on under side. 8 feet.

1 gallon	8	.50	.55
5 gallon	35	1.50	1.65

Gardenia fortunei.............................FORTUNE GARDENIA

Has large double white fragrant flowers. This is the ever-bloom-
ing variety. Excellent for an unusual hedge. It can be most satis-
factorily used as a tub plant in climates where it will not survive
the winter; or it is cheap enough that replacements can be made
each spring. It is useful as an annual in those areas. Always a
good seller. 6 feet.

1 gallon	8	.40	.45
5 gallon	35	1.00	1.10
15-18 in.	22	.50	.55
18-24 in.	30	.75	.85
24-30 in.	40	1.00	1.10
30-36 in.	70	1.35	1.50

Gardenia mystery..........................MYSTERY GARDENIA

A favorite variety with the florist. Not hardy in Northeast Texas.
6 feet.

1 gallon	8	.40	.45
18-24 in.	30	.75	.85
24-30 in.	40	1.00	1.10

CHINESE HORNED HOLLY - 1 gallon

Ilex cornuta..............................CHINESE HORNED HOLLY
Very stiff, bright, glossy green holly leaves gracefully curved.
Large red berries add to its attractiveness. 15 feet.

	Weight	10 or More F.O.B. Nursery	F.O.B. Dallas Less than 10 at Nursery
1 gallon sdlgs or ctgs.	8	.80	.85
5 gallon	35	1.75	1.90
15-18 in.	22	1.50	1.65
18-24 in.	30	2.00	2.20

BURFORD HOLLY - 1 gallon

Ilex cornuta burfordi............BURFORD CHINESE HOLLY

Dark glossy green stiff leaves with one tip spine forming a very smooth appearance; large red berries. Our most popular holly. 8 feet.

	Weight	10 or More F.O.B. Nursery	F.O.B. Dallas Less than 10 at Nursery
1 gallon	8	.80	.85
1 gallon Berried	8	1.00	1.10
5 gallon	35	1.50	1.65
15-18 in.	30	1.50	1.65
18-24 in.	30	2.00	2.20

Ilex crenata rotundifolia...............JAPANESE HOLLY

Splendid dark green spineless holly with round leaves. For formal plantings or makes a fine, low hedge. A good substitute where other than Boxwood is desired. Black berried variety but ours are purposely propagated from male plants and are nonfruiting. Hardy in Northern and Eastern states. 3 feet.

1 gallon	8	.60	.65
12-15 in.	14	1.00	1.10
15-18 in.	22	1.35	1.50

Ilex hume No. II...............HUME HYBRID AMERICAN HOLLY

A cross between American and Dahoon hollies resulting in a holly tree similar in general appearance to the Christmas Holly, but being more prolific in berry production. Leaves are lighter colored than American Holly. 25 feet.

5 gallon	35	1.75	1.90
30-36 in.	40	1.75	1.90

Ilex Opaca................AMERICAN HOLLY

Very hardy native tree with medium green oval leaves surrounded by evenly spaced short spines on the edge. Red berries. 50 feet.

5 gallon limited supply	35	1.75	1.90

Ilex vomitoria................YAUPON HOLLY

A great favorite for hedges. Bright red berries. 15 feet.

15-18 in.	30	1.20	1.30
18-24 in.	40	1.50	1.65

Ilex cassine................DAHOON HOLLY

A tree holly with willow-like leaves; fruits abundantly at a young age with bright red berries from fall until spring. 20 feet.

1 gallon	8	.60	.65
5 gallon	35	1.75	1.90
2 - 3 ft berried	30	2.00	2.20
3 - 4 ft. berried	40	2.50	2.65
2 - 3 ft. not berried	30	1.75	1.90
3 - 4 ft. not berried	40	2.00	2.20

Jasminum nudiflorum...............WINTER JASMINE

Generally the earliest flowering of the yellow Jasmines and hardiest. 3 feet.

15-18 in.—B&B	22	.50	.55
18-24 in.—B&B	30	.70	.80
24-30 in.—B&B	40	1.00	1.10

Jasminum primulinum...............PRIMROSE JASMINE

Large yellow flowers, bush vigorous, gracefully arching. Less hardy than other varieties. 8 feet.

1 gallon	8	.40	.45
18-24 in.—B&B	30	.70	.80
2 - 3 ft.—B&B	40	1.00	1.10

Jasminum humile...............FLORIDA JASMINE

The most versatile and popular of the Jasmine family. Flowers through most of the summer after a profusion of blossoms in the spring. A most attractive plant. 4 feet.

1 gallon	8	.50	.55
15-18 in.	22	.60	.70
18-24 in.	30	1.00	1.10
24-30 in.	40	1.50	1.65

Laurocerasus caroliniana.........................CHERRY LAUREL

Since this plant is subject to loss of foliage when transplanted container grown stock is all the more valuable. Our field plants are young and have been rootpruned so they should transplant with less difficulty than the average. This is an exceptionally good plant for hedge work. It responds to shearing as well as any tree. 12 feet.

	Weight	10 or More F.O.B. Nursery	F.O.B. Dallas Less than 10 at Nursery
1 gallon	8	.50	.55
5 gallon	35	1.50	1.65
18-24 in.	30	1.00	1.10
24-30 in.	40	1.25	1.35
30-36 in.	40	1.50	1.65
3 - 4 ft.	70	2.00	2.20
4 - 5 ft.	70	2.50	2.75

Lavendula vera..TRUE LAVENDER

To vary the color scheme in a planting, this is the hardy perennial to use. Lavender sachets are made from the flowers and seeds of this low growing symmetrical little plant. Very fragrant gray color herb. Blue flowers. Good for low borders. The True English Lavender. 2 feet.

6 -12 in.	22	.60	.65
12-15 in.	22	.90	1.00

Leucophyllum texanum..SENISA

Sage like shrub. Abundant orchid colored flowers after every summer rain. Dwarf variety. Compact grower. 5 feet.

1 gallon	8	.50	.55
5 gallon	35	1.50	1.65

Ligustrum japonica.............................JAPANESE PRIVET

Evergreen, good for tall hedges. Fast growing, easy to transplant. 20 feet.

1 gallon	8	.40	.45
5 gallon	35	1.25	1.35
2 - 3 ft.	30	1.00	1.10
3 - 4 ft.	40	1.35	1.50

WAXLEAF LIGUSTRUM - 1 gallon

Ligustrum lucidum compactum............WAXLEAF PRIVET

Dense compact glossy dark green leaves, grows to 6 feet in height and horizontally the same but requires some shearing to keep it symmetrical. 6 feet.

1 gallon	8	.55	.60
5 gallon	35	1.50	1.65
15-18 in.	22	.55	.60
18-24 in.	30	1.00	1.10
24-30 in.	40	1.50	1.65

Lonicera yunannensis......................YUNNAN (ROSEGLO)
HONEYSUCKLE

Dwarf but relatively fast growing -- semi prostrate shrub with
small dark leaves; pink flowers. Most attractive. 3 feet.

	Weight	10 or More F.O.B. Nursery	F.O.B. Dallas Less than 10 at Nursery
1 gallon	8	.60	.65

Loropetalum chinensis............SOUTHERN WITCHHAZEL

Formerly known as Chinese White Fringe Shrub. New, half dwarf
evergreen shrub. Covers itself with white feathery flowers in
earliest spring and a few flowers occasionally in summer and fall.
One of the few lesser size good shrubs seeking better acquaintance
and wider use. 3-5 feet.

1 gallon	8	.50	.55
5 gallon	35	1.50	1.65

SOUTHERN
WAX MYRTLE - 1 gallon

MAGNOLIA - 1 gallon

Magnolia grandiflora....................SOUTHERN MAGNOLIA

Very large and handsome dark green glossy leaves with the familiar
huge fragrant white blossoms make these trees a thing of majes-
tic beauty. 50 feet.

1 gallon	8	.50	.55
5 gallon	35	1.50	1.65
18-24 in.	30	1.00	1.10
2 - 3 ft.	40	1.50	1.65
3 - 4 ft.	70	2.00	2.20

Mahonia bealei........................LEATHERLEAF MAHONIA

This plant is most desirable because it fills so well the need for
shaded areas. It thrives in shade but will take some sun if for a
short period of time during the day, preferably in the morning.
Large shiny, gray-green leaves with spines make this plant un-
usually appealing. Also large clusters of yellow flowers followed by
blue grape like seed pods add to its sales appeal. 3 feet.

1 gallon	8	.50	.55
5 gallon	35	1.25	1.35
15-18 in.	22	1.00	1.10
18-24 in.	30	1.50	1.65

Myrica cerifera........................SOUTHERN WAXMYRTLE,
BAYBERRY

Leaves spicily fragrant. Bears blue Cedar-like berries on trunk
and base of branches which, with its shiny leaves and spiciness,
make it very useful and attractive. A hardy evergreen which will
survive Missouri cold, West Texas heat and East Texas wet and
humid conditions. 10 feet.

1 gallon	8	.60	.65
5 gallon	35	1.35	1.50

	Weight	10 or More F.O.B. Nursery	F.O.B. Dallas Less than 10 at Nursery

Myrtus communis microphylla............DWARF ROMAN MYRTLE

A dwarf shrub compact in growth. Glossy dark green leaves, white fragrant flowers. Good for low hedges or edgings. 18 inches.

1 gallon	8	.45	.50

NANDINA - 1 gallon

Nandina domestica..NANDINA

This cane-like shrub with its small dainty and light green summer foliage is an accepted 'must' with gardeners because of the gorgeous leaf coloring in the fall and immense clusters of red berries which are retained throughout the winter. 8 feet.

1 gallon	8	.50	.55
5 gallon	35	1.35	1.50
15-18 in.	22	.80	.90
18-24 in.	30	1.35	1.50

Photinia serrulata..PHOTINIA

Large, holly-like, dark green foliaged ornamental evergreen shrub. 15 feet.

1 gallon	8	.50	.55
5 gallon	35	1.50	1.65
18-24 in.	30	1.00	1.10
24-30 in.	40	1.35	1.50
30-36 in.	40	1.75	1.90
3 - 4 ft.	70	2.00	2.20

Pittosporum tobira......................................PITTOSPORUM

Well known dark green, elongated heavy leaved, slow growing round evergreen shrub. 5 feet.

1 gallon	8	.50	.55
5 gallon	35	1.25	1.35
15-18 in.	22	.75	.85
18-24 in.	30	1.00	1.10

Podocarpus..JAPANESE YEW

The only edition of the popular yew family of plants suitable for the Southwest. 20 feet.

1 gallon	8	.50	.55
5 gallon	35	1.50	1.65

Pyracantha Graber, Henderson, Barlow, Miller................RED BERRIED FIRETHORN

Large evergreen shrub with glossy foliage and huge clusters of large red berries. Wonderful for cash and carry sales. 8 feet.

1 gallon	8	.80	.85
5 gallon staked	35	1.75	1.90

Pyracantha lalandi........................LALAND FIRETHORN
Upright growing; orange fruits early in fall. Well known. Makes
a brilliant show until late winter. Hardier than Red varieties.
10 feet.

	Weight	10 or More F.O.B. Nursery	F.O.B. Dallas Less than 10 at Nursery
1 gallon	8	.70	.75
5 gallon	35	1.50	1.65

—

VINES

Ampelopsis brevipedunculata elegans............PORCELAIN
VINE
Very ornamental, tendril-climbing shrub or vine; leaves brightly
variegated green, white and pink. Splash of spring and fall colors.

1 gallon	8	.35	.40

Antigonon leptopus...CORAL VINE,
QUEEN'S WREATH
A fast growing vine for summer shade. Will produce 30-40 ft.
of vines in one season. Vines are not hardy. Plant dies back to
tuber each fall. Large clusters of coral colored flowers in abundance
all summer.

1 gallon	8	.40	.45

GELSEMIUM - I gallon   PITTOSPORUM - I gallon

Gelsemium sempervirens.....................CAROLINA JASMINE
Tubular yellow, pleasantly fragrant flowering vine.

1 gallon staked	8	.50	.55
5 gallon staked	35	1.00	1.10

Hedera helix..ENGLISH IVY
Dark green leaves with prominent white veining. The original
English Ivy.

1 gallon	8	.40	.45

Lonicera halleana.........................HALL'S HONEYSUCKLE
White climbing vine. Flowers June to October. Fast grower, evergreen. 25 feet.

1 gallon staked	8	.35	.40
15-18 in. Bareroot		.25	.30
18-24 in. Bareroot		.40	.45
2 - 3 ft. Bareroot		.60	.65
15-18 in.—B&B	22	.50	.55
18-24 in.—B&B	30	.65	.70
2 - 3 ft.—B&B	30	.80	.90

HALL'S HONEYSUCKLE - 1 gallon

Lonicera heckrotti..............HECKROTT HONEYSUCKLE
Flame; everblooming; semi-evergreen.

	Weight	10 or More F.O.B. Nursery	F.O.B. Dallas Less than 10 at Nursery
18-24 in. Bareroot		.50 .	.55
2 - 3 ft. Bareroot		.70	.75
18-24 in.—B&B	30	.70	.80
2 - 3 ft.—B&B	40	1.00	1.10

Lonicera sempervirens...............................RED CORAL OR
   SCARLET TRUMPET HONEYSUCKLE
Everblooming, red; usable as either shrub or vine.

5 gallon 35		1.00	1.10
18-24 in. Bareroot		.45	.50
2 - 3 ft. Bareroot		.70	.75
18-24 in.—B&B	30	.70	.80
2 - 3 ft.—B&B	40	1.00	1.10

Wistaria chinensis...............................CHINESE WISTARIA
Propagated from plants which bloom before the leaves appear.
Makes a gorgeous spring display of wistaria flowers.

1 gallon 8		.40	.45
1 yr. No. 2 Bareroot		.20	.23
1 yr. No. 1 Bareroot		.30	.35
3 yr. No. 1 Bareroot		.50	.55
3 yr. Jumbo young tree form Bareroot		.90	1.00

Euonymus radicans colorata.................WINTERCREEPER
Ground cover for shady places. Fine for terrace walls and build-
ings. 8 ft. spread.

15-18 in. Bareroot		.20	.23
18-24 in. Bareroot		.30	.33
2 - 3 ft. Bareroot		.40	.45

DECIDUOUS SHRUBS & TREES

Albizzia julibrissin..............................PINK MIMOSA TREE
Wide spreading lawn tree. Pink flowers all summer. Fern-like
foliage. 20 feet.

1 gallon 8		.35	.40
5 gallon 35		1.00	1.10
2 - 3 ft. Bareroot ....—		.20	.23
3 - 4 ft. Bareroot ....—		.35	.40
4 - 5 ft. Bareroot ....—		.50	.55
5 - 6 ft. Bareroot ....—		.70	.80
6 - 8 ft. Bareroot ....—		1.00	1.10
8 -10 ft. Bareroot ....—		1.50	1.65

MIMOSA - 1 gallon

Albizzia julibrissin alba................WHITE MIMOSA TREE
Same as above but white flowers.

	Weight	10 or More F.O.B. Nursery	F.O.B. Dallas Less than 10 at Nursery
1 gallon	8	.40	.45
2 - 3 ft. Bareroot	—	.30	.33
3 - 4 ft. Bareroot	—	.45	.50
4 - 5 ft. Bareroot	—	.65	.70

Berberis thunbergi atropurpurea...........JAPANESE RED-
LEAF BARBERRY
Well known ornamental. Dark red stems and foliage.

1 gallon	8	.45	.50

Cercis canadensis...............................AMERICAN REDBUD
Light green, heart shaped leaves which are preceded in the spring
by lavender-pink blooms all along the branches. Used extensively
for highway, street and park beautification. 25 ft.

1 gallon	8	.40	.45
2 - 3 ft. Bareroot	—	.20	.23
3 - 4 ft. Bareroot	—	.35	.40
4 - 5 ft Bareroot	—	.50	.55
5 - 6 ft. Bareroot	—	.75	.85
2 - 3 ft.—B&B	.40	.40	.45
3 - 4 ft.—B&B	.40	.55	.60
4 - 5 ft.—B&B	.70	.75	.80
5 - 6 ft.—B&B	.70	1.00	1.10

Cercis chinensis...CHINESE REDBUD
A dwarf variety branching heavily from the ground forming a
bush rather than a tree. Flowers and leaves are closer together on
branches. 5 feet.

1 gallon	8	.40	.45

Exochorda grandiflora.................................PEARL BUSH
Pearl-like buds, white flowers. January, February and March.
Should be moved early. 10 feet.

5 gallon	35	1.00	1.10
2 - 3 ft.—B&B	30	.75	.85
3 - 4 ft.—B&B	40	1.10	1.20
4 - 5 ft.—B&B	70	1.50	1.65

Heteropteris .... REDWING
Shrub with striking red colored terminals similar to winged maple
seeds. 3 feet.

1 gallon	8	.50	.55
5 gallon	35	1.20	1.30

HYDRANGEA & ENGLISH IVY - I gallon

Hydrangea .... **HYDRANGEA**

The hardy outdoor Hydrangea which yields a great mass of white, pink and blue flowers (color depending on the type of soil) in the early summer months. 4 feet.

	Weight	10 or More F.O.B. Nursery	F.O.B. Dallas Less than 10 at Nursery
1 gallon	8	.50	.55
5 gallon	35	1.25	1.35

Lagerstroemia indica.................................**CRAPEMYRTLE**

One of the few midsummer flowering shrubs. It is covered with a gorgeous array of bloom heads; flowers are produced the first summer on new growths and may be increased in size from year to year by an annual fall pruning. Needs little or no care and is unrivaled for its colorful beauty in any situation, formal, naturalistic, specimen or group plantings. Often called the Southern Lilac. Red. 10 feet.

1 gallon	8	.40	.45
5 gallon	35	.75	.85
2 - 3 ft. Bareroot	—	.30	.25

Ligustrum amurensis........**AMUR RIVER SOUTH PRIVET**

Used almost entirely for hedges, but can be sheared into any desired shape. Globes, pyramids and cones are easily made and sell well. 10 feet.

18-24 in. Bareroot—per 100	8.00	8.50
24-30 in. Bareroot—per 100	10.00	10.50
30-36 in. Bareroot—per 100	12.00	12.50
3 - 4 ft. Bareroot—per 100	15.00	16.00

Liquidambar styraciflua........................**SWEET GUM TREE**

Deep rich green five pointed leaves which in the fall enhance any landscape with their assorted bright colors. Also the burrs or seed pods are ornamental in flower decorations. 50 feet.

5 gallon	35	1.10	1.20
5 - 6 ft.—B&B	70	2.00	2.20
6 - 8 ft.—B&B	110	2.50	2.75
8 -10 ft.—B&B	160	3.50	3.85

Melia umbraculiformis........**CHINESE UMBRELLA TREE**

A very popular southern shade tree. Umbrella in general appearance and one of densest shades available. 15 feet.

1 gallon	8	.40	.45
5 gallon	35	1.00	1.10

Salix babylonica pendula........................**WEEPING WILLOW**

The universally known weeping favorite. 20 feet.

5 gallon	35	1.00	1.10

Spirea prunifolia..............................PLUMLEAVED SPIREA

Glossy foliage resembling plum leaves. Flowers are small but double and without limit. A very graceful shrub. 5 feet.

	Weight	10 or More F.O.B. Nursery	F.O.B. Dallas Less than 10 at Nursery
2 - 3 ft. Bareroot ....—		.30	.33
3 - 4 ft. Bareroot ....—		.50	.55

Spirea billardi................................BILLARD SPIREA

A 6-8 inch long spike-like flower from spring into midsummer. Flowers are wine color and a little bit fuzzy. A good cut flower. Very different but useful.

2 - 3 ft. Bareroot ....—		.25	.28
3 - 4 ft. Bareroot ....—		.35	.40

Spirea Reevesi flore pleno........................REEVES SPIREA

This is the real white double flowering Bridal Wreath. 6 feet.

1 gallon 8		.50	.55
18-24 in. Bareroot ....—		.30	.35
24-30 in. Bareroot ....—		.40	.45
30-36 in. Bareroot ....—		.50	.55

Ungnadia speciosa................................SPANISH BUCKEYE

Pretty pea-like lavender flowers early on a nice shrub. Black buckeyes. Nice novelty, 6 feet.

3 - 4 ft. Bareroot ....—		.80	.90
4 - 5 ft. Bareroot ....—		1.25	1.35

Wistaria chinensis..............................CHINESE WISTARIA, TREE FORM

Propagated from plants which bloom before the leaves appear. Makes a wonderful spring display. Should be dug and delivered early while dormant, preferably by February 1st., as the flower buds shatter off during later delivery.

2 - 3 ft.—B&B 40		2.25	2.50
2 - 3 ft.—B&B Heavy....40		2.75	3.00
3 - 4 ft.—B&B 70		3.25	3.50
4 - 5 ft.—B&B 110		3.75	4.25

GRASSES

Cortaderia argentea.................................PAMPAS GRASS

Clumps of giant grass which bend into a fountain effect and send up huge white foamy plumes that are outstandingly attractive. 6 feet.

1 gallon 8		.40	.45
5 gallon 35		.75	85

Close-Up View of WAXLEAF and MAGNOLIAS in I Gallon Cans.

JUNIPERS IN ONE-GALLON CANS

CONTAINER GROWN STOCK

The introduction of Container Grown or Canned Plants is relatively new in our Southwest area. Nevertheless its rapid acceptance by the Nursery trade and general public proves its practical value.

Canned Plants are helping in a large way to make the landscape business a year round enterprise rather than seasonal as heretofore. Canned Plants are taking the slump out of salesyards also. An attractive display of plants throughout the summer will pay for the operation of a retail yard and bring profit to the owner as well.

Plants growing in cans can be harvested in any kind of weather. A truck can be loaded without notice of its coming, and the stock moves without loss.

We list our can stock separately for your convenience. All items listed here are also shown under the main list where descriptions are given.

VARIETY—	Size	F.O.B. Scottsville	F.O.B. Dallas
Abelia	1 gallon	.50	.55
Abelia	5 gallon	1.25	1.35
Arborvitae, Baker	1 gallon	.50	.55
Arborvitae, Excelsa	1 gallon	.45	.50
Arborvitae, Rosedale	1 gallon	.45	.50
Barberry Julianne	1 gallon	.35	.40
Barberry Mentorensis	1 gallon	.60	.65
Boxwood Harland	1 gallon	.50	.55
Boxwood English	1 gallon	.50	.55
Camellia Sasanqua	1 gallon	.70	.75
Camellia Sasanqua	5 gallon	1.60	1.75
Cedar Deodar	1 gallon	.60	.65
Cedar Deodar	5 gallon	1.60	1.75
Cedar Incense	5 gallon	1.50	1.65
Cherry Laurel	1 gallon	.50	.55
Cherry Laurel	5 gallon	1.50	1.65
China Berry	1 gallon	.40	.45
China Berry	5 gallon	1.00	1.10
Crepe Myrtle	1 gallon	.40	.45

VARIETY—	Size	F.O.B. Scottsville	F.O.B. Dallas
Crepe Myrtle ....5 gallon		.75	.85
Cypress, Arizona ....1 gallon		.50	.55
Cypress, Italian ....1 gallon		.45	.50
Eleagnus Simoni ....5 gallon		1.25	1.35
Euonymus, Japanese ......1 gallon		.40	.45
Gardenia, Fortune ....1 gallon		.40	.45
Gardenia, Fortune ....5 gallon		1.00	1.10
Gardenia, Mystery ....1 gallon		.40	.45
Holly, American ....1 gallon		.65	.70
Holly, American ....5 gallon		1.75	1.90
(limited supply)			
Holly, Burford ....1 gallon		.80	.85
Holly, Burford Berried ..1 gallon		1.00	1.10
Holly, Chinese Horned ....1 gallon		.80	.85
Holly, Chinese Horned ....5 gallon		1.75	1.90
Holly, Dahoon ....1 gallon		.60	.65
Holly, Dahoon ....5 gallon		1.75	1.90
Holly, Hume ....1 gallon		.65	.70
Holly, Hume ....5 gallon		1.75	1.90
Holly, Japanese ....1 gallon		.60	.65
Honeysuckle, Hall's ....1 gallon		.35	.40
(staked)			
Honeysuckle, Red Coral ..5 gallon		1.00	1.10
Honeysuckle, Yunnan ....1 gallon		.60	.65
Hydrangea ....1 gallon		.50	.55
Hydrangea ....5 gallon		1.25	1.35
Jasmine, Carolina ....1 gallon		.50	.55
(staked)			
Jasmine, Carolina ....5 gallon		1.00	1.10
Jasmine, Humile ....1 gallon		.50	.55
Jasmine, Primrose ....1 gallon		.40	.45
Juniper, Ashford ....1 gallon		.40	.45
Juniper, Irish ....1 gallon		.45	.50
Juniper, Irish ....5 gallon		1.20	1.30
Juniper, Kiyono ....1 gallon		.60	.65
Juniper, Shore ....1 gallon		.50	.55
Juniper, Spiny Greek ......1 gallon		.60	.65
Juniper, Sylvestris ....1 gallon		.50	.55
Ligustrum, Japanese ......1 gallon		.40	.45
Ligustrum, Japanese ......5 gallon		1.25	1.35
Ligustrum, Waxleaf ......1 gallon		.55	.60
Ligustrum, Waxleaf ......5 gallon		1.50	1.65
Loropetalum ....1 gallon		.50	.55
Loropetalum ....5 gallon		1.50	1.65
Magnolia, Southern ....1 gallon		.50	.55
Magnolia, Southern ....5 gallon		1.50	1.65
Mahonia Leatherleaf ....1 gallon		.50	.55
Mahonia Leatherleaf ....5 gallon		1.25	1.35
Myrtle, Roman Dwarf ....1 gallon		.45	.50
Myrtle, Southern Wax ....1 gallon		.60	.65
Myrtle, Southern Wax 5 gallon		1.35	1.50
Mimosa, Pink ....1 gallon		.35	.40
Mimosa, Pink ....5 gallon		1.00	1.10
Mimosa, White ....1 gallon		.40	.45

VARIETY—	Size	F.O.B. Scottsville	F.O.B. Dallas
Nandina	1 gallon	.50	.55
Nandina	5 gallon	1.35	1.50
Pampas Grass	1 gallon	.40	.45
Pearl Bush	5 gallon	1.00	1.10
Pineapple Guava	1 gallon	.50	.55
Pineapple Guava	5 gallon	1.50	1.65
Pine, Loblolly	1 gallon	.40	.45
Photinia	1 gallon	.50	.55
Photinia	5 gallon	1.50	1.65
Pittosporum	1 gallon	.50	.55
Pittosporum	5 gallon	1.25	1.35
Podocarpus	1 gallon	.50	.55
Podocarpus	5 gallon	1.50	1.65
Porcelain Vine	1 gallon	.35	.40
Pyracantha, Red (staked)	1 gallon	.80	.85
Pyracantha, Red	5 gallon	1.50	1.65
Pyracantha, Orange	1 gallon	.70	.75
Pyracantha, Orange	5 gallon	1.50	1.65
Queen's Wreath	1 gallon	.40	.45
Redbud, American	1 gallon	.40	.45
Redbud, Chinese	1 gallon	.40	.45
Redwing	1 gallon	.50	.55
Redwing	5 gallon	1.20	1.30
Senisa	1 gallon	.50	.55
Spirea Billiard	1 gallon	.35	.40
Spirea Reeves double	1 gallon	.50	.55
Sweet Gum	5 gallon	1.10	1.20
Weeping Willow	5 gallon	1.00	1.10
Wistaria, Chinese	1 gallon	.40	.45

WISTARIA - 1 gallon

For Customer's Convenience and Satisfaction Cut All Cans Before They Leave the Retail Sales Yard.

THE "REDHEAD" CAN SHEAR

The best instrument made for cutting cans off plants. Built for durability and simplicity. Saves time, saves hands, saves tempers. $6.75 each, freight extra.

CPSIA information can be obtained
at www.ICGtesting.com
Printed in the USA
BVHW091238261118
534010BV00012B/244/P